OH, THE WILD JOYS OF LIVING!

ROBERT BROWNING

MORE

DO MORE OF WHAT MAKES YOU FEEL ALIVE

———————————

WRITTEN BY: KOBI YAMADA ○ DESIGNED BY: JILL LABIENIEC

LIFE IS SO MUCH MORE.

Big, meaningful, wholehearted living is so much more than just measuring up, moving on, or getting by. It is looking forward, leaning in, and feeling alive. It is doing things like chasing a dream, connecting with friends, making a difference, and being inspired. Why not see the possibilities in each moment that are waiting to be discovered? Because the beautiful thing is that every day is filled with these magical moments and each of those moments contains endless opportunities for something good, something special, something more.

WHY NOT HAVE A BIG LIFE?

UNKNOWN

MORE

EVERY SUNRISE IS AN INVITATION FOR US
TO ARISE AND BRIGHTEN SOMEONE'S DAY.

RICHELLE E. GOODRICH

GET MORE INVOLVED

DO SOMETHING WONDERFUL,
PEOPLE MAY IMITATE IT.

ALBERT SCHWEITZER

CARE
MORE

...A LIFE
SPENT
LOVING...
IS A LIFE
WELL
SPENT.

SUZANNE CLOTHIER

EVERYTHING YOU
WANT IS ON THE
OTHER SIDE OF FEAR.

JACK CANFIELD

AGE

EXPECT
MORE

ALWAYS
BELIEVE THAT
SOMETHING
WONDERFUL
IS ABOUT TO
HAPPEN.

UNKNOWN

TOUCH. BE GENEROUS. PAY ATTENTION. OPEN Y
GIVE BACK. MAKE SOMEONE'S DAY. WORK TOGE
RY TO UNDERSTAND. CELEBRATE THE DIFFERE
AMILY. GIVE THANKS. SHARE YOUR SMILE. PRA
OUR PASSION. KEEP IN TOUCH. BE GENEROUS.
PONTANEOUS. HAVE FUN. GIVE BACK. MAKE SC
CIATE THE LITTLE THINGS. TRY TO UNDERSTAN
RIENDS. TREAT FRIENDS LIKE FAMILY. GIVE TH
ESPECT. BE ROMANTIC. FIND YOUR PASSION. K
OUR HEART. FALL IN LOVE. BE SPONTANEOUS.
GETHER. CARE DEEPLY. APPRECIATE THE LITTLE
NCES. TREAT FAMILY LIKE FRIENDS. TREAT FRI
RACTICE KINDNESS. SHOW RESPECT. BE ROMA
OUS. PAY ATTENTION. OPEN YOUR HEART. FALL
OMEONE'S DAY. WORK TOGETHER. CARE DEEPI
TAND. CELEBRATE THE DIFFERENCES. TREAT F/
HANKS. SHARE YOUR SMILE. PRACTICE KINDNI
EEP IN TOUCH. BE GENEROUS. PAY ATTENTION
HAVE FUN. GIVE BACK. MAKE SOMEONE'S DAY. V
LE THINGS. TRY TO UNDERSTAND. CELEBRATE
RIENDS LIKE FAMILY. GIVE THANKS. SHARE YO

HEART. FALL IN LOVE. BE SPONTANEOUS. HAV
R. CARE DEEPLY. APPRECIATE THE LITTLE THIN
S. TREAT FAMILY LIKE FRIENDS. TREAT FRIENDS
CE KINDNESS. SHOW RESPECT. BE ROMANTIC. F
ATTENTION. OPEN YOUR HEART. FALL IN LOVE
ONE'S DAY. WORK TOGETHER. CARE DEEPLY. AP
ELEBRATE THE DIFFERENCES. TREAT FAMILY LI
S. SHARE YOUR SMILE. PRACTICE KINDNESS. SH
IN TOUCH. BE GENEROUS. PAY ATTENTION. OP
E FUN. GIVE BACK. MAKE SOMEONE'S DAY. WOR
INGS. TRY TO UNDERSTAND. CELEBRATE THE
S LIKE FAMILY. GIVE THANKS. SHARE R SMI
C. FIND YOUR PASSION. DEEPLY. TOUCH. BE GEN
OVE. BE SPONTANEOUS. HAVE FUN. GIVE BACK
PPRECIATE THE LITTLE THINGS. TRY TO UNDER
LY LIKE FRIENDS. ECT FRIENDS LIKE FAMILY.
SHOW RESPECT BE RO ANTIC. YOUR PAS
EN YOUR HEART. FALL IN LOVE. BE SPONTANE
K TOGETHER. CARE DEEPLY. APPRECIATE THE
DIFFERENCES. TREAT FAMILY LIKE FRIENDS. T
MILE. PRACTICE KINDNESS. SHOW RESPECT

LOVE MORE

MORE
GENER

THE MEANING OF LIFE IS
TO FIND YOUR GIFT.
THE PURPOSE OF LIFE
IS TO GIVE IT AWAY.

DAVID VISCOTT

OSITY

LISTEN MORE CLOSELY

WHEN YOUR HEART
SPEAKS, TAKE GOOD NOTES.

JUDITH CAMPBELL EXNER

FEEL
MORE

BE IN LOVE WITH YOUR LIFE, EVERY MINUTE OF IT.

JACK KEROUAC

MORE GRATITUDE:

APPRECIATE
EVERYONE AND
EVERYTHING
IN YOUR LIFE.

WAYNE DYER

MORE

HAPP

<blockquote>
LIFE IS MEANT TO
BE FUN, AND JOYOUS,
AND FULFILLING.

JIM HENSON
</blockquote>

NESS

APPRECIATE MORE

THERE IS BEAUTY IN EVERYTHING...

HELEN KELLER

MORE
PURPOSE

IF YOU COULD
ONLY SENSE HOW
IMPORTANT YOU
ARE TO THE LIVES OF
THOSE YOU MEET...
THERE IS SOMETHING
OF YOURSELF THAT
YOU LEAVE AT EVERY
MEETING WITH
ANOTHER PERSON.

FRED ROGERS

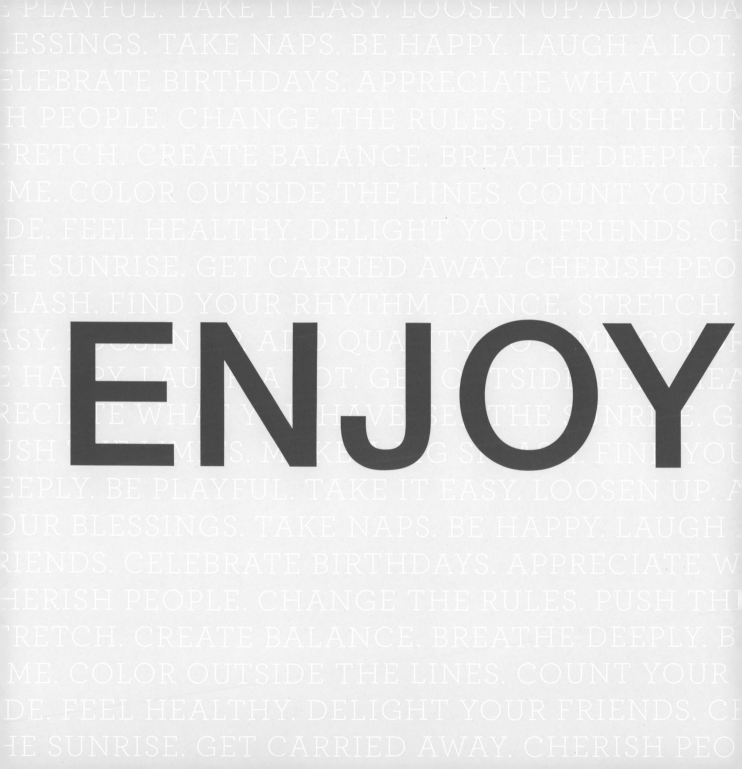

MAKE MORE TIME FOR THE GOOD THINGS

I STILL FIND EACH DAY TOO
SHORT FOR ALL THE THOUGHTS
I WANT TO THINK, ALL THE
WALKS I WANT TO TAKE, ALL THE
BOOKS I WANT TO READ, AND
ALL THE FRIENDS I WANT TO SEE.

JOHN BURROUGHS

MORE
PASSI

LET THE BEAUTY OF
WHAT YOU LOVE BE
WHAT YOU DO.

RUMI

ON

NOTICE
MORE

ISN'T IT FUNNY
HOW DAY BY
DAY NOTHING
CHANGES, BUT
WHEN YOU
LOOK BACK,
EVERYTHING IS
DIFFERENT...

C. S. LEWIS

THERE IS NOTHING IN THE WORLD SO IRRESISTIBLY CONTAGIOUS AS LAUGHTER AND GOOD HUMOR.

CHARLES DICKENS

MORE JOY

HAPPINESS IS AVAILABLE.
PLEASE HELP YOURSELF TO IT.

THÍCH NHẤT HẠNH

DO MORE OF WHAT YOU LOVE

FIND SOMETHING YOU'RE PASSIONATE ABOUT AND KEEP TREMENDOUSLY INTERESTED IN IT.

JULIA CHILD

MORE

WHAT DID YOU DO AS A CHILD THAT
MADE THE HOURS PASS LIKE MINUTES?

CARL JUNG

SEE MORE

ER BEEN. TAKE CHANCES. WELCOME NEW THIN
AVE. SPREAD JOY. FOLLOW YOUR CURIOSITY. R
RSELF. TAKE A VACATION. MAKE NEW FRIENDS.
AD LIGHTLY. LOOK FOR THE GOOD. GO HAND I
REACH OUT. GO WHERE YOU'VE NEVER BEEN. T
. GET LOST. KEEP AN OPEN MIND. BE BRAVE. SPI
IES. ENJOY THE JOURNEY. SEE FOR YOURSELF.
NDER. LEARN A NEW LANGUAGE. TREAD LIGHT
AVEL EVERYWHERE. ASK QUESTIONS. REACH O
THINGS. TAKE THE SCENIC ROUTE. GET LOST.
TY. RIDE A BIKE. MAKE MEMORIES. ENJOY THE J
DS. EXPLORE NEW LANDS. WANDER. LEARN A NI
HAND. TAKE ROAD TRIPS. TRAVEL EVERYWHERE
AKE CHANCES. WELCOME NEW THINGS. TAKE
READ JOY. FOLLOW YOUR CURIOSITY. RIDE A BI
E A VACATION. MAKE NEW FRIENDS. EXPLORE N
LOOK FOR THE GOOD. GO HAND IN HAND. TAK
GO WHERE YOU'VE NEVER BEEN. TAKE CHANCE
EP AN OPEN MIND. BE BRAVE. SPREAD JOY. FOL
OURNEY. SEE FOR YOURSELF. TAKE A VACATION
W LANGUAGE. TREAD LIGHTLY. LOOK FOR THI

EXPLORE MORE

I HAVEN'T BEEN EVERYWHERE, BUT IT'S ON MY LIST.

SUSAN SONTAG

...THE WORLD IS
INCOMPREHENSIBLY
BEAUTIFUL—AN ENDLESS
PROSPECT OF MAGIC
AND WONDER.

ANSEL ADAMS

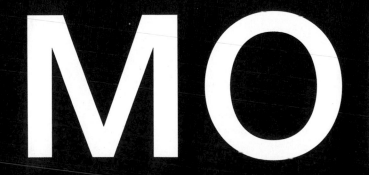

MORE

TAKE MORE CHANCES

"IT'S IMPOSSIBLE," SAID PRIDE.
"IT'S RISKY," SAID EXPERIENCE.
"IT'S POINTLESS," SAID REASON.

"GIVE IT A TRY,"
WHISPERED THE HEART.

UNKNOWN

MAKE MORE HAPPEN

ONE DAY YOU WILL WAKE UP AND THERE WON'T BE ANY MORE TIME TO DO THE THINGS YOU'VE ALWAYS WANTED. DO IT NOW.

PAULO COELHO

THIS IS THE BIG TIME...

ANNIE DILLARD

LEARN SOMETHING NEW. HAVE FUN. TRUST YOU
ES. TAKE CHANCES. BE SILLY. HAVE ADVENTUR
Y. ENJOY SIMPLE PLEASURES. EMBRACE NEW ID
OLUNTEER. USE YOUR IMAGINATION. WELCOME
AY CURIOUS. DO WHAT YOU'VE ALWAYS WANT
RUST YOUR INSTINCTS. MAKE EVERY MOMENT
DVENTURES. BE SPONTANEOUS. GET INVOLVED
RACE NEW IDEAS. PLANT A SEED. GET YOUR HA
ON. WELCOME NEW CHALLENGES. LOOK UP. TH
WAYS WANTED TO DO. FEEL ALIVE. LEARN SOM
VERY MOMENT COUNT. MAKE MEMORIES. TAKE
ET INVOLVED. FIND YOUR CREATIVITY. ENJOY S
OUR HANDS DIRTY. GIVE FREELY. VOLUNTEER. U
P. THINK BIG. LIGHT THE WAY. STAY CURIOUS. D
ARN SOMETHING NEW. HAVE FUN. TRUST YOU
ES. TAKE CHANCES. BE SILLY. HAVE ADVENTUR
Y. ENJOY SIMPLE PLEASURES. EMBRACE NEW ID
OLUNTEER. USE YOUR IMAGINATION. WELCOME
AY CURIOUS. DO WHAT YOU'VE ALWAYS WANT
RUST YOUR INSTINCTS. MAKE EVERY MOMENT
DVENTURES. BE SPONTANEOUS. GET INVOLVED

LIVE MORE

COMPENDIUM®
live inspired

WITH SPECIAL THANKS TO THE ENTIRE COMPENDIUM FAMILY.

CREDITS:
Written and Compiled by: Kobi Yamada
Designed by: Jill Labieniec
Edited by: M.H. Clark, Kristin Eade, and Amelia Riedler
Creative Direction by: Julie Flahiff

PHOTOGRAPHY CREDITS:

Front cover, pages 35, 41, 60-61: no more lookism / photocase.com; pages 1, 23, 64: misterQM / photocase.com; pages 2-3, 53: steko7 / photocase.com; pages 4-5: mariolagrobelska.de / photocase.com; page 9: Sonne-13 / photocase.com; pages 11, 43: faniemage / photocase.com; pages 14-15: hajos / photocase.com; page 21: felix-g / photocase.com; pages 24-25: GabiPott / photocase.com; page 29: Seleneos / photocase.com; pages 31, 38-39: eskemar / photocase.com; page 45: rowan / photocase.com; pages 50-51: particula / photocase.com; page 57: en.joy.it / photocase.com; page 59: melrose / photocase.com.